# Sleeping to Save Energy

SRA

Columbus, OH

# SRAonline.com

 **SRA**

The McGraw-Hill Companies

Black bear eating berries

## Saving Energy

All animals need energy to live. An animal's normal body functions, such as breathing, moving, and digesting food, use energy. Energy lets the heart pump blood. Energy lets the intestines digest food. Animals, like people, get energy from the foods they eat. Bears get their energy from a diet of berries and fish. Squirrels get energy from grains, seeds, and nuts.

How does energy get into these foods? First, a plant absorbs sunlight through its leaves. The plant uses energy from the sun to make glucose, which is a type of sugar. Some of this sugar is stored in the plant.

When an animal eats the plant it takes in this stored glucose. The animal's body absorbs the glucose. The body then converts it into the energy it needs to move, eat, and breathe. These processes are called metabolism. Some of this energy is also stored to use later.

This process is similar to the way the engine of a car works. When fuel is put into a car the engine converts it into energy to power the car. The fuel that isn't used waits in the gas tank to be used later.

Eating for energy is easy when there is lots of food around. This is not always the case. Two things affect an animal's ability to survive when winter comes.

First, cold weather makes it difficult to find food. Many plants that animals eat don't grow in winter. Animals must then rely on the food they stored in their bodies in the fall. If they run out of this food they will not survive. Second, an animal's metabolism uses more energy in cold weather. It does this to keep a constant body temperature. When it is cold outside, animals use up more energy to stay warm.

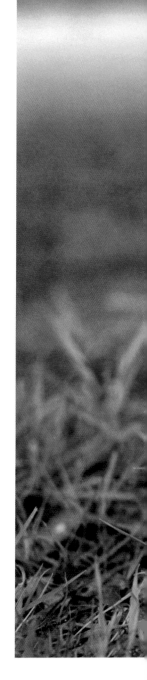

Squirrel eating a nut

## A Special Kind of Sleep

Animals in cold climates adapt so they can survive the harsh weather. One way some adapt is hibernation. When animals hibernate they go into a special kind of deep sleep. They live mostly off the food stored in their bodies. While they are hibernating their bodies change in ways that make sure the animals use less energy. If they use less energy they need less food. Through hibernation the animal is able to live through times when food is scarce.

Although hibernation sounds simple, it involves more than just a wintertime nap. Scientists have studied what really happens to hibernating animals.

As the weather grows cold, animals that hibernate get ready for the long months ahead. They eat more food than usual, storing up a thick layer of fat. During their long sleep they use this fat for energy. Some animals are able to survive the winter using only this fat. They also put on a layer of special fat called "brown fat" near their heart, liver, and brain.

Other hibernating animals store food in addition to their extra fat. They gather nuts, seeds, and berries and hide them in their burrows and dens. In these cozy spots the animals are protected from severe cold and hungry predators.

Squirrel stocking up on acorns before winter

When an animal hibernates its metabolism slows. Normal body temperature for most mammals is around 99°F. When they hibernate this number falls below 50°F. Most animals breathe many times per minute. Their hearts beat quickly too. But when they hibernate everything slows down. A woodchuck's heart beats seventy-five times per minute when it is awake. When it hibernates its heart rate is only about four beats per minute. And an arctic ground squirrel may take as few as two breaths per minute when hibernating!

It might seem like a hibernating animal is nearly dead. People who see one might not be able to tell the difference between hibernation and death.

Black bear mother and cubs coming out of den

## Who Hibernates, and How?

Most people think that bears hibernate in the winter. According to scientists, this is not true. Bears sleep for long periods during cold weather but they do not really hibernate. As the weather, turns colder bears look for dens to protect themselves from winter weather. Some dens are in caves. Others can be in hollow tree stumps or in a hole at the base of a large tree.

Scientists know that bears do not really hibernate in winter because a bear's body temperature does not drop. On warmer days, bears get up, move around, and find food to eat.

In contrast, ground squirrels and woodchucks are animals that do truly hibernate. An arctic ground squirrel is one example of a hibernator. During the coldest months these animals curl up to sleep in underground nests. Their body temperatures drop almost to the freezing point—32°F. During this time they can lose up to half their body weight. They wake up only once or twice a month to have a bite to eat from the food they've stored in their nests. They hibernate for seven or eight months. That's over half of the year!

You may know when it's time to go to sleep because you have a set bedtime or you feel sleepy.

Scientists think that several events start hibernation in animals. One trigger, or something that starts a process, is colder temperatures. Another trigger is shorter days and longer nights. As winter approaches there are fewer hours of daylight. When days are shorter there is less time to find food. And when nights are longer, animals that sleep when it is dark have more time to do so.

The change in seasons triggers hibernation.

When one or more of these events happen a natural chemical enters the animal's blood. This is called *hibernation induction trigger,* or HIT.

HIT slows the heart rate and other body functions. HIT also protects the cells that make up the animal's tissues and organs. This way, organs such as the heart and brain remain unharmed during the cold months of winter.

Scientists are still learning about what HIT can do. Some scientists have taken blood containing HIT from hibernating squirrels. When they injected this blood into active squirrels, the active squirrels immediately began to hibernate!

## Awake and Alive

How do you wake up in time for school each morning? Perhaps an alarm clock goes off at a certain time. Maybe a parent wakes you up. But have you ever woken up just because you were not sleepy anymore or because you were hungry? When that happens your natural body rhythm is telling you what to do, just like an alarm clock.  Animals' bodies have natural rhythms that act as alarm clocks too. Hibernating animals instinctively wake up when the weather gets warmer so their bodies can get the food they need after a long winter.

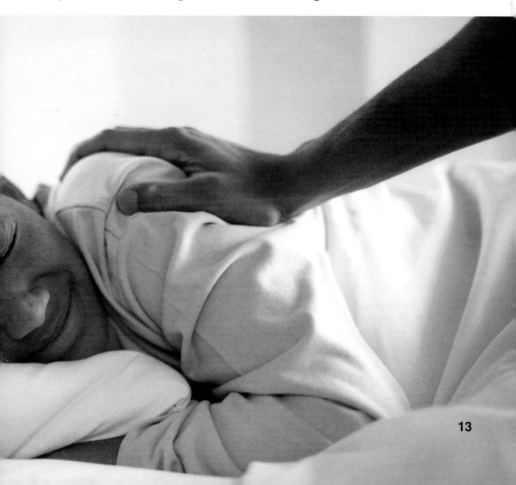

**Arctic ground squirrels**

One of the first things an animal's body does to wake up from hibernation is raise its temperature. To do this it may shiver to create heat. The brown fat that was stored near the animal's organs is converted into heat. This warms the heart, liver, and other important organs

quickly.

It takes a while for animals to get back to normal after hibernating. When they first wake up they are unsteady. They are weak and slow because they have lost most of their body fat. This makes them easy prey for predators, so they must be cautious.

When you first wake up in the morning you are probably groggy. Then you gradually become alert. Animals waking after hibernation are the same. After a while they are fully awake and alert again. They return to their normal sleep habits. They also return to their regular diet. In only a few days they reach a normal body weight. After months of hibernation they wake in spring, able to find plenty of food again. They have survived a cold winter with very little food by sleeping to save energy.

# Vocabulary

**diet** (dī´ it) (page 3) *n.* The food and drink eaten by an animal.

**absorbs** (əb sorbz) (page 3) *v.* Takes in.

**converts** (kən vûrts´) (page 4) A form of the verb **convert:** To change something into something different.

**layer** (lā´ ər) (page 6) *n.* One thickness of something.

**predators** (pre´ də tərz) (page 6) *n.* Plural form of **predator:** An animal that hunts and kills other animals for food.

**alert** (ə lûrt´) (page 15) *adj.* Awake and prepared to act.

# Comprehension Focus: Summarizing

1. Summarize what happens to an animal's body during hibernation.

2. Summarize how hibernation helps an animal survive in the winter.